ECUMENISM 101

ECUMENISM 101

A Handbook about the Ecumenical Movement

By Alton M. Motter

FORWARD MOVEMENT PUBLICATIONS
Cincinnati, Ohio

This book is warmly

DEDICATED

— To those pioneers of YESTERDAY—who laid the foundations for greater Christian unity, as well as for the unity of all of God's children.

— To those who are actively carrying that responsibility TODAY—amid a fast changing world.

— To those prophetic voices to come—who will blaze new pathways for God's better world TOMORROW.

CONTENTS

INTRODUCTION

"Where can I find a short, readable book for lay persons which gives the basic facts about the ecumenical movement?"

The search to find an answer to that question led to the writing of this short volume.

It is true that, during this century, noted scholars, theologians, and church historians have written thick volumes dealing with the history and the various theological developments and dialogues related to the ecumenical movement. But few of these ever reach the men and women in the pew.

There is a place, therefore, for a basic primer which will answer the most logical questions interested lay persons ask about this movement which has helped to make, as one writer has called it, an "ecumenical century."

Consequently, I asked 35 representative laity, including some experienced ecumenical leaders, from about a dozen denominations, to name the kinds of questions they would like answered.

The answers are based upon this writer's four decades of ecumenical service and leadership with councils of churches at local, metropolitan, state, national, and world levels. Naturally, those insights have been greatly sharpened and refined by the experiences and writings of many others.

Let me add these very personal lines:

My life span has covered most of this ecumenical century. I was born three years before the famous Edinburgh Missionary Conference of 1910.

As I selected my first list of 10 ecumenical pioneers in Appendix A, I realized that I knew seven of the 10, and had worked closely with four.

The ecumenical highlight of my career was undoubtedly my attendance at Vatican II. It was with deep humility and gratitude that I knelt before the tomb of Pope John XXIII, and prayed for the greater fulfillment of his ecumenical vision, as well as for the prayer of our Lord, that the greater oneness of God's church may be more fully realized.

With these lines, I pass the ecumenical torch to you, the reader. If you can respond, I hope you will carry it wisely and well.

To be sure, we cannot see the end of this turbulent pilgrimage. But, as we are reminded by Reinhold Niebuhr: "Nothing that is worth doing can be achieved in one lifetime." The ecumenical movement is "worth doing." It will require many lifetimes. May yours be one of them.

Alton M. Motter
The Day of Pentecost
May 26, 1996

BEGINNINGS:
The seed is sown

1. Just what is the ecumenical movement all about?

The ecumenical movement is basically concerned with developing greater understanding and appreciation between all Christians, which will lead to greater mutual cooperation and visible unity. Such unity, its leaders believe, is God's will, and is acknowledged as a gift from God in the person of Jesus Christ.

2. What do the words "ecumenism" and "ecumenical" mean?

The word "ecumenism" is a noun derived from two Greek words *oikoumene* ("the inhabited earth") and *oikos* ("house"). Ecumenism could be understood as, "The people of the whole world who live within a common house."

When traced to the teachings and prayers of Christ, ecumenism is used to describe the worldwide household of those who hold to one Christian faith and becomes a key word for the movement for greater Christian understanding, appreciation, and visible unity.

The word "ecumenical" is an adjective used to describe this 20th century movement and its leadership.

In the broadest sense, both words can also relate not only to the more visible unity and mission of all Christians but also to the unity of humankind.

3. What are some New Testament references which motivate the search for interchurch cooperation and Christian unity?

In the New Testament, the writers of the four Gospels and the letters of the Apostle Paul call for harmony and love between the followers of Christ. While differences of interpretation and emphasis developed during the New Testament period, Christians were called to be servants of reconciliation in resolving differences.

4. How did Jesus express his concern for the future unity of his followers?

He stated this very clearly during the Lord's Supper with his disciples. In what is usually called his "New Commandment," he said:

"I give you a new commandment, that you love one another. Just as I have loved you, you should also love one another. By this everyone will know that you are are my disciples, if you have love for one another" (John 13:34-35).*

Then, during his prayer for his disciples at that supper, he prayed that they "may all be one . . . that the world may believe" (John 17:21).

5. What did the Apostle Paul have to say about the way Christians should relate to one another?

Paul was equally emphatic in calling for Christ-like love to mark the relationship between Christians. He defined the nature of that love in the classic 13th chapter of his First Letter to the Corinthians. Nearly all of his letters contain references to the way Christians are to relate to one another.

To the Romans he wrote: "Love one another in mutual affection; outdo one another in showing honor" (Romans 12:10).

To the Ephesians he said: "We are members of the household of God." Christians were to be so joined together that they would grow together to form a holy temple for which Christ would be the cornerstone (Ephesians 2:19-22).

Paul said that just as the various organs of the human body must function in harmony, so Christians should work together as members of the Body of Christ (1 Cor. 12:12-31).

---

*All Biblical quotations are from the New Revised Standard Version.

Perhaps Paul's strongest call for Christian unity came when he heard about the divisions which had taken place in the Christian community in Corinth:

"Now I appeal to you, brothers and sisters, by the name of our Lord Jesus Christ, that all of you be in agreement, and that there be no divisions among you, but that you be united in the same mind and the same purpose.

"For it has been reported to me by Chloe's people that there are quarrels among you, my brothers and sisters.

"What I mean is that each of you says, 'I belong to Paul,' or 'I belong to Apollos,' or 'I belong to Cephas,' or 'I belong to Christ.'

"Has Christ been divided? Was Paul crucified for you? Or were you baptized in Paul's name?" (1 Cor. 1:10-17).

6. Does the ecumenical movement seek to establish one "super-church" for all Christians?

No, it does not. But it does seek to establish a more visible unity of Christ's church in the world. Isn't it fair to say that our excessive Christian divisions in America, and throughout the world, have greatly hampered Christ's mission for his church?

FOR DISCUSSION

- What was your understanding of ecumenism and the ecumenical movement before you read this book?

- How do your friends or other church members feel about this movement?

- In what ways does the New Testament support and undergird the ecumenical movement?

GROWTH:
Century of explosion

7. What led to the rise of the modern ecumenical movement?

In the U.S. the movement began with lay-oriented Bible and mission societies in the east. Later, evangelistic "camp meetings" developed in the midwest. Other interdenominational and non-denominational movements such as antislavery, temperance, foreign missions, and youth work, helped to pave the way for many Christians to work together across denominational lines.

One of the most significant factors in the growth of interdenominational work in this country, however, was in the area of religious education.

As the nation expanded, there was a great need for Sunday school teachers and curriculum materials. This led to the establishment of Sunday school associations which were formed by lay volunteers at the county, state, and national levels.

The basic mission of these associations was to promote the teachings of the Bible, especially among children and youth, for the purpose of leading them to a commitment to Christ as Lord and Savior.

The author's outlook toward other denominations and the mission of the church was greatly influenced by these conventions in the 1920s which he attended as an older adolescent.

These associations laid the groundwork for many of the federations and councils of churches which followed.

An example of these stages of interdenominational cooperation is portrayed by these organizational steps which took place in the area of Buffalo, N.Y.:

1857 - The Erie County Sabbath School Association
1863 - The Erie County Sunday School Association
1911 - The Inter-Church Missionary Union
1913 - The Buffalo Federation of Churches
1930 - The Council of Churches of Buffalo & Erie County
1971 - The Buffalo Area Council of Churches.

Similar evolving changes took place in such states as Minnesota, Indiana, and Ohio as well as in other states.

Interdenominational developments also took place as college and university students met to pray and plan together. These student developments, which took place in both this country and throughout the world in the middle and late 1800s, led to the formation of the YMCA, the YWCA, and the student Christian movements (SCMs). These movements furnished many leaders for the ecumenical movement.

8. What are some of the early significant U.S. dates and events related to Christian unity?

Nationally, the movement toward greater church cooperation in the U.S. was highlighted by the formation of the Federal Council of Churches in 1908. Made up of representatives of 29 Protestant denominations, the Federal Council developed strong positions in matters related to social justice, especially as the industrial revolution was making its impact upon American society. Some state councils, however, preceded the Federal Council before the turn of the century.

The Federal Council was replaced in 1950 by the National Council of the Churches of Christ in the U.S.A. (NCCC). The council continued to be supported by the mainline Protestant churches and an increasing number of Orthodox bodies. It also brought together a variety of other national interdenominational agencies. These had worked in the areas of Christian education, refugee assistance, racial justice, justice for women, stewardship, disaster response, and overseas services to meet many human needs in more than 70 countries.

The council also included a theological study unit called Faith and Order to deal with Christian unity. Later, it developed offices dealing with Christian-Jewish and Christian-Muslim relations. In 1996, the NCCC had 32 Protestant, Anglican, and Eastern Orthodox church bodies. While the Roman Catholic Church is not a member, this church participates in some of the work of the NCCC and cooperates in a variety of units and ecumenical programs.

9. Is the ecumenical movement also a worldwide movement?

It is indeed! This movement truly forms a broad ecumenical fabric. Christian congregations and church bodies seek to attain a greater degree of Christian unity and to work together at every level of church and community life, from the neighborhood to the world.

10. What led to the formation of the world council of churches?

The most significant event which led to the foundation of the World Council of Churches took place in 1910 when the Protestant and Anglican churches from around the world sent 1,200 delegates to a meeting initiated by the International Missionary Council in Edinburgh, Scotland. Their deep concern was to reduce denominational competitiveness and to make Christ known to the millions who had not heard the Gospel.

Pastor Marc Boegner of France was deeply sensitive to the divisive effects of denominationalism as he recalled these words of a participant from Asia:

"You have brought us your divisions. We beg you to preach the Gospel to us, and allow Jesus Christ to raise up, through his Spirit, a church set free of all the 'isms' that now influence your preaching of the Gospel among us."

Most scholars recognize this International Missionary Conference as the beginning of the modern ecumenical movement. A Christian Conference on Life and Work was organized in 1925 at Stockholm, Sweden. It attempted to deal with some of the issues of peace and justice between nations.

In 1927, the first World Conference on Faith and Order—so named because it dealt with basic Christian beliefs and how the churches structure (order) their worship, sacraments, and ministry—was held in Lausanne, Switzerland. On that occasion, steps were taken to overcome historic misunderstanding to establish deeper theological dialogues among the churches in order to clear the way for a greater degree of Christian unity.

These three streams of international church life eventually flowed together in today's World Council of Churches. The WCC was organized in 1948 at Amsterdam in the Netherlands when 351 representatives from 147 church bodies were present from 44 nations. Earlier plans for the formation of the council had been postponed because of World War II.

These leaders formed an instrument whereby the churches would more effectively bear witness in their common allegiance to Christ, search for that unity which they believed God wills for the church, and cooperate in matters of common concern and responsibility.

11. To What Extent Was the Modern Missionary Movement Especially Responsible for the Rise of the Ecumenical Movement?

The ties between the Christian missionary movement and the ecumenical movement are very deep. As the various missionaries faced similar problems and sometimes competed with one another in different parts of the world, they soon came to realize that "A divided church can never win the world for Jesus Christ." Consequently, under the leadership of men like John R. Mott, the missionary-evangelism impulse which gave rise to the ecumenical movement was especially strong.

12. Was a concern for ecumenism expressed in earlier centuries of Christian church history?

Yes. It was expressed at various times and in many ways. One writer has said that major divisions have taken place in the Christian church about every 500 years.

After each separation, steps were taken to heal the causes and results of such divisions. As the Christian faith continued to expand, however, this healing became more difficult.

Changing political boundary lines, the nature of different ethnic cultures, problems associated with language translations, the rise of competing nationalisms, and long delays caused by extremely slow methods of communication and transportation, all added to these difficulties. None of these earlier efforts was notably successful.

13. Who were some of the great pioneers in the ecumenical movement?

Though there were many, the author names 10 who are listed in Appendix A. There are many other influential men and women who helped to shape the movement for greater Christian unity and church cooperation.

14. Just how widespread is the ecumenical movement in the world today?

During this "ecumenical century," the ecumenical movement has spread far and wide. The number of member church bodies in the World Council of Churches, for example, has more than doubled since its founding. It now includes 324 members located in more than 100 nations. Included are many church bodies in Africa, Asia, Latin America, the Middle East, and the South Pacific in addition to the European and North American churches which formed the basic membership in 1948.

15. Do the various assemblies of the world council of churches help tell the story of the worldwide outreach of the ecumenical movement?

They do indeed. Held about every seven years, the assemblies are attended by some 1,000 delegates who are selected by their member church bodies. Attendance sometimes includes as many as three times that many visitors! These gatherings have been called the most representative gatherings of the Christian church since the first century. In a sense, they form a modern Pentecost.

During these assemblies the delegates and visitors who speak many languages can, with the assistance of modern translation facilities, share in common worship, study the Bible together, receive reports on wider ecumenical developments in the world, evaluate the many ministries which have been carried out in various nations since the previous assembly, seek a common mind on selected contemporary issues, determine future goals in keeping with God's vision of peace and justice, and elect WCC presidents and members of its central committee.

16. When and where have these assemblies been held?

The dates, locations, and themes have been as follows:

Country	Year	Theme
1. Amsterdam, The Netherlands	1948	"Man's Disorder and God's Design"
2. Evanston, Illinois, U.S.A.	1954	"Christ—The Hope of the World"
3. New Delhi, India	1961	"Jesus Christ—The Light of the World"
4. Uppsala, Sweden	1968	"Behold I Make All Things New"
5. Nairobi, Kenya	1975	"Jesus Christ—Frees and Unites"

| 6. Vancouver, Canada | 1983 | "Jesus Christ—The Life of the World" |
| 7. Canberra, Australia | 1991 | "Come, Holy Spirit, Renew the Whole Creation" |

The next WCC assembly will be held in 1998 in Harare, Zimbabwe, when the theme will be "Turn To God; Rejoice In Hope."

FOR DISCUSSION

- Why do you think some writers call this the ecumenical century?

- In what ways did the pioneer conditions in the U.S. contribute to this movement?

- How would you describe the missionary roots of the ecumenical movement?

SIMILARITIES:
Things we have in common

17. What do most Christians in the world have in common?

Christians confess Jesus Christ as their Lord and Savior. That is the strongest common tie among all the world's Christians.

As we reflect upon the elements of the Christian faith, and its historical developments, we should also recognize these 10 elements which we could share in common:

1. An active faith in Christ, and the challenge to follow his teachings.

2. The recognition of the cross as a common symbol of the Christian faith.

3. The authority and use of the Bible as a spiritual resource, and of the New Testament as a more specific guide for Christian living.

4. The use of the Apostles' and/or the Nicene Creed(s) as a historical confession of the Christian faith.

5. The praying of the Lord's Prayer as Jesus' model prayer for speaking to God.

6. The recognition of baptism as an initiation to the Christian life and incorporation into full membership in Christ's church.

7. The sharing of the Lord's Supper—The Eucharist—as commanded by Jesus.

8. The singing of Christian hymns from many ethnic and denominational sources.

9. The acceptance of others—regardless of

ethnic, racial, economic, educational or cultural differences—as members of the human family.

10. The promise and assurance of eternal life,
based upon the Resurrection of Christ.

18. Are Christians today moving toward a more common approach in their study of the Bible?

In many respects, yes. The vast number of new Bible
translations which have appeared in recent years is a great
asset. English-speaking Christians are no longer limited to
the King James translation of 1611. Many Christians hold
to a word-to-word literal acceptance of the Bible. Other Christians have a more historical and structural understanding
of how the Bible came to be. Still, the work of our Bible
scholars and the new Bible translations are helping to
establish a more comprehensive approach to our fuller
understanding of the Bible. This has helped to strengthen
the ecumenical movement.

19. To what extent is there a growing agreement on the meaning of baptism among Christians today?

There is a strong and growing tendency for most denominations to accept each other's baptism. When performed with
water in the name of the Trinity such a baptism is accepted,
for example, by Roman Catholic and Eastern Orthodox
churches, as well as by many Protestant churches, including
some Baptists. Pastors in some denominations, for whom
"believers' baptism" is primary, however, may not do so, and
may require a second baptism, frequently by immersion.

Readers desiring to explore a serious ecumenical study
on this topic will find assistance in the 33-page document
"Baptism, Eucharist, and Ministry" which reflects a wide and
growing consensus by churches throughout the world on these
important aspects of the Christian faith.

A study guide, "Growing Together in Baptism, Eucharist, and Ministry," could also be quite helpful.

20. Is there a growing openness among Christians in their observances of the Lord's Supper?

To some degree. Many Protestant churches have had a long-standing "open communion" policy which welcomes all Christians. Those who wish to renew the spirit and presence of Christ in their lives are invited to receive the Holy Communion elements in their services.

Some denominations, such as the Lutheran, Episcopal and Reformed churches, are completing theological studies which may result in a broader sharing of eucharistic practices among them.

The Roman Catholic Church and Eastern Orthodox churches have what might be called a "limited" eucharistic policy. This means that there can be a shared communion under certain circumstances. Their leaders hold that there should be a common agreement with other Christians concerning the faith and unity of the church before a broader policy can be accepted. Most other churches believe that a common sharing in this holy sacrament of Christ bears witness to and creates the unity which Christ has already established and to which he is leading us.

21. To what extent are the historic Christian creeds accepted by most Christians today?

A growing number of churches are using the Apostles' and/or the Nicene Creed(s) as a historical summary of the Christian faith. This recognizes that when these creeds were finally approved, between about 325 and 700 AD, they contained the basic teachings of the church, as the Christian faith was understood and interpreted at that time.

In more recent times, however, a number of modern creeds or "affirmations of faith" were developed, such as those included in the 1989 edition of the United Methodist Hymnal.

These spell out more clearly some aspects of the Christian faith and Christian discipleship not articulated in the classical historical creeds.

Some denominations, such as the Presbyterian Church, USA, and the United Church of Christ, have developed even more contemporary and challenging statements of the Christian faith.

22. Is there a common English translation of the Lord's Prayer used by all Christians today?

The answer is clearly "not yet!" For example, some denominations continue to use the phrase, "Forgive us our debts, as we forgive our debtors." Others say, "Forgive us our trespasses as we forgive those who trespass against us." A later translation, developed by the International Consultation on English Texts, uses "Forgive us our sins, as we forgive those who sin against us." A growing number of churches now use this later translation. But identical words are not required for it to be the Lord's Prayer. This ecumenical consultation also made helpful changes in the wording of the Apostles' and Nicene Creeds.

23. Can our Christian hymns contribute to ecumenical awareness?

By all means! As we sing hymns, most of us are not aware of the wide and varied denominational roots of our hymn writers and composers. Without realizing it, we sing ecumenically.

At Christmas, for example, we all join in singing "O Little Town of Bethlehem" by Episcopalian Phillips Brooks, "Hark! The Herald Angels Sing" by Methodist Charles Wesley, "Joy to the World" by Anglican Isaac Watt, "Silent Night" by Roman Catholic Joseph Mohr, and "Go Tell It on the Mountain," the African American spiritual—without ever asking, "What was the denomination of the hymn writer?"

24. Is it now possible for pastors of different traditions to participate in interchurch marriages?

Increasingly. This is especially true in recent years for Protestant-Roman Catholic marriages. An increasing number of guidelines for mixed marriage preparations and celebrations are being developed by bishops and pastors of different denominations.

One example of such guidelines, developed by Roman Catholic, Lutheran and Episcopalian leaders in Pennsylvania, provides helpful guidance for such marriage plans and is available for study and use.

No longer is it so often necessary for families to become divided by mixed marriages, as was common only a few decades ago.

Such arrangements are not generally carried out, however, with Eastern Orthodox priests.

An unusually challenging treatment of how interchurch marriages can relate to the cause of Christian unity is given in a book, *Double Belonging: Interchurch Families and Christian Unity.*

FOR DISCUSSION

- Do you agree with the 10 expressions of the Christian faith which the author proposes should be comon to all Christians?

- Which translation of the Lord's Prayer do you prefer? Why?

- In spite of different theological interpretations of the Lord's Supper, can it have a meaningful value to most Christians? If so, what is it?

DIFFERENCES:
Crossing boundary lines

25. What accounts for the many differences within Christianity today?

These differences are difficult to explain briefly. Basically, they are rooted in history:

1. Early differences arose about the nature of Jesus: Was he entirely human, entirely divine, or both human and divine? These differences had a long history preceding the adoption of the classical creeds.

2. Christianity expanded from its Jewish beginnings in Jerusalem and Palestine to a wider Greek and Gentile culture. This led to differences among Christians which were sometimes deep, and always challenging.

3. As this expansion moved into what is now Greece and Turkey, and then later into Syria, Persia, Egypt, and North Africa, differences developed concerning some interpretations of the Christian faith and liturgical forms of worship, but especially about the supreme authority in the church.

Centuries of differences led in 1054 to the great schism, or division, between the Christians of the East and Christians of the West.

One sign of the continuing differences between these major branches of Christianity is their inability to agree on a common date for observing Easter, the chief festival in the Christian year.

4. In northern Europe, the Protestant Reformation came to a focus in Martin Luther in 1517. This was caused by abuses within the Western Church of that day and by differing concepts related to the means of salvation. Other cultural developments were also taking place as a rising nationalism was emerging in Europe.

The Reformation resulted in many new separations: Lutherans in Germany and later in the Scandinavian countries; Mennonites and other Anabaptists in Germany, Switzerland and Holland; Reformed and Presbyterians in Switzerland, Scotland, and part of France; Anglicans and Baptists in England during the 18th century. During the two centuries between 1500 and 1700 many other denominations developed.

26. Why are there so many different denominations in the U.S.?

The answer may be four-fold:

1. While Native Americans were here first, the early settlers who came from all parts of Europe brought their different religious beliefs and practices with them. As people arrived later from other regions of the world, they did the same.

2. Though some of the original 13 colonies had established official religious policies, these policies were eventually replaced when the Constitution of the U.S.A. prohibited the establishment of any official church, such as existed in Europe. This meant that every religious body would have equal standing before the government, both state and national.

3. Complete individual freedom to worship God, according to the dictates of one's conscience—or not to worship, or to change one's religious affiliation—was provided for every citizen. This meant also the freedom to start new religious groups.

Consequently, when a member or a group was not in agreement with a church's theological doctrines, or interpretations of the Bible, or found its practices discriminatory—African Americans often did—they were free to start a new church. A great many have done so, for reasons both great and small.

4. The absence of a centralized teaching authority such

as existed in the Roman Catholic Church also made it possible for many new groups and churches to be established.

Today there are 208 U.S. denominations listed in the 1996 Yearbook of American and Canadian Churches. Even then, not all church groups are listed there, since many are very small, and some do not wish to be so listed.

Because of these factors, we may well be the most religiously diverse country in the world, and our Christian churches present a richly diverse plurality.

27. What are the general groupings of Protestants in the U.S.?

Most Protestants, but not all, are related to about 17 church "families."

While many denominations in these groupings are members of the National and World Councils of Churches, some belong to the National Association of Evangelicals and/or the World Evangelical Fellowship. Some belong to neither.

28. Do different Catholic traditions also exist today?

Yes. One such body in this country is the Polish National Catholic Church of America. A few others use the word Catholic in their identification, but are not recognized by the Roman Catholic Church.

29. To what extent do we have a variety of Orthodox Church bodies in the U.S.?

Twenty such bodies are known in the U.S. Most of their names reflect an early Christian rootage traced to Greece and a variety of eastern European or Middle East countries such as Armenia, Bulgaria, Romania, Russia, Syria and the Ukraine, as well as North Africa. While they belong to Eastern Orthodox and Oriental Orthodox confessional families, they have achieved a high degree of mutual respect and cooperation in this country.

30. What accounts for the vast differences in worship patterns of our various denominations and traditions?

These many patterns seek to reflect reverence and communication with God, and are generally related to the cultural and historical backgrounds of our respective church bodies.

There are deep differences between the worship pattern of a Roman Catholic church, for example, and that which takes place in a Friends meeting house; between that which occurs in a Lutheran or an Episcopal church and that in a Baptist or a Pentecostal church; between a service in a traditional African American church and an Orthodox church. Yet, all seek to communicate with the same God.

Nearly all churches use scriptures, prayers, sermons or homilies, music, hymns, symbols and symbolic acts to lead the worshiper into a closer relationship with God.

One of the unfinished goals of the ecumenical movement is to deepen our understanding, appreciation, and respect for each other's worship patterns which are tending to become more similar among some denominations.

31. How should one address clergy persons of different religious traditions?

Perhaps the most common term is "pastor" which means "shepherd"—one who cares for our spiritual well being and growth. Indeed, bishops in some denominations carry a shepherd's crook or staff as a symbol of their office.

While Roman Catholic, Orthodox and some Episcopalian clergy prefer to be called "father," or "mother" in the Episcopal Church, many do not object to being called "pastor."

Presbyterians and Methodists generally seem to prefer "minister"—to reflect the theme of Jesus as expressed in an earlier translation of Matthew 20:28: "I came not to be ministered to, but to minister."

Some other clergy persons prefer to be called "evangelist"

or in some specialized cases "chaplain" or "sister" or "brother." Still others simply desire to be called "Mr." or "Miss," "Mrs.," or "Ms." The use of the term "reverend" is generally discouraged, as is the word "preacher." The importance of the specific title, however, is not so much a matter of "what is right" but "what shows respect" for the office in the ministry of a particular denomination.

32. Have attempts been made to bring the different world religions together?

Yes, to some extent. This, however, is a gigantic task. If we accept the concept of the broad term "religion" as being the "search for meaning," we include many types of responses in the history of the human race.

SOME OF THE WORLD'S MAJOR RELIGIONS

Name & When Founded	Supreme Being	Founder	Approximate Adherents
1. Hinduism 3200 BC	Brahman	No historical founder	764,000,000
2. Judaism 1300 BC	Yahweh (God)	Abraham	13,451,000
3. Taoism 604 BC	Jade Emperor (many folk gods)	Lao-Tzu	31,389,000
4. Confucianism 557 BC	Confucius	Confucius	6,334,000
5. Buddhism 525 BC		Gautama Buddha	338,621,000

6. Christianity 30 AD	God	Jesus	3,723,277,000
7. Islam 622 AD	Allah (God)	Mohammad	1,033,453,000
8. Shintoism 720 AD	Izanagi (Sky Father)	No historical founder	3,387,800
9. Baha'i 1836 AD	God	Baha'ullah	5,835,000

In spite of the difficulties involved in trying to bring the leaders of all the religions of the world together for a common purpose, several attempts have been made. Two of these related to the resolve to eliminate war.

The first was the formation of the World Alliance for Promoting International Friendship Through the Churches which was formed in Switzerland on August 2, 1914—one day after World War I erupted. The delegates were forced to leave for their homes on August 3. In spite of that, however, an ecumenical pioneer peace association was established to face international problems.

In 1929, a decade after the war, some 500 World Alliance delegates met in the city of Prague. They agreed to urge people of all countries to work for a rapid and universal reduction of all armaments, to adopt methods of arbitration and mediation in the settlement of all international disputes, and to support wholeheartedly the work of the League of Nations.

While the alliance dissolved two decades later, its work of advocating peaceful resolution of conflicts, disarmament, and international reconciliation was passed to the World Council of Churches' Commission of the Churches on International Affairs and its program on Dialogue with Persons of Other Faiths and Idealogies.

During the period following 1914 and the end of WWI, a second effort resulted in creation of the Church Peace Union. This was established by Protestant, Roman Catholic, and Jewish leaders who also worked to include leaders of other religious faiths for the cause of peace.

More recently, a world conference on religion and peace has been formed.

33. Have other efforts been made to bring all of the world's religious faiths together?

Yes. Probably the first inclusive effort was the World's Congress of Religions held in Chicago in 1893. Held during the World's Columbian Exposition to mark the 400th Anniversary of Christopher Columbus's first journey to the Americas, this brought 400 representatives of 10 major religions of the world from over a dozen countries.

While no specific steps were taken to establish long-ranging interfaith relationships, some scholars feel that the congress (a) gave an impetus to the comparative study of the history of religion, (b) helped to give rise to the interfaith movement, and (c) may have contributed indirectly to the beginning of the ecumenical movement.

A century later, in 1993, a second World's Congress of Religions was held, in Chicago and in Bangalore, India. In contrast to the first Congress, some 6,000 participants were present from more than 125 religious groups who took part in nearly 700 lectures, panel discussions, dances, and musical events.

One observer reported that, compared to the more optimistic mood in 1893, the 1993 Chicago gathering was marked by a deeper mood of anxiety.

That anxiety was expressed in its final "Declaration of a Global Ethic," which was regarded as an initial step in "applying ancient principles to current world problems." The declaration stated that these "ancient principles condemned the inequalities in the world economy; environmental abuse;

sensationalism and political manipulation in the mass media; sexual discrimination; and religiously-fueled violence." The closing speaker, the Dalai Lama from Tibet, said to the thousands gathered in Chicago's Grant Park: "If we are to have spiritual harmony, we must accept the existence of different religions."

34. What is the basis for the criticisms sometimes leveled against the U.S. National Council and the World Council of Churches?

Such criticisms usually come from one of two sources. The first is from those who hold a different theological perspective. They usually call for a specific way of interpreting the Bible, and insist upon a more detailed statement of what should be included in defining those who may be called Christians. They fear the goal is either a super-church imposing its authority on all, or one in which deep differences do not matter.

The churches participating in Christian councils of churches, on the other hand, feel that the acceptance of Jesus Christ as Lord and Savior is a sufficient base for working with fellow believers for greater Christian unity and cooperation. They feel that different understandings of the Bible, and more detailed refinements of theology, should be left to each church and denomination according to its scholarship and tradition.

The second source of criticism has been from those who resisted the implications of Christ's Gospel for some of the larger social and economic needs of society. They believed the task of the church was only to bring people to Christ and found it difficult to see how or why the Christian Gospel should question some national, economic and political policies, as they may relate to such issues as poverty, racism and violence. That attitude is now changing.

Council leaders, on the other hand, made up of denominational representatives, feel there are times when all human systems fall under God's judgment, and cry out for the presence of Christ's love. As in the case of Peter and the early disciples, they say, "We must obey God, rather than a human authority" (Acts 5:2a).

The solution for honest differences is to be found in open and genuine dialogue rather than through confrontation and expressions of ill will against one another.

FOR DISCUSSION

- How many churches of other denominations, within the general radius of your church, can you name? What do you know about them?

- It has been said that at least 95 percent of us are members of a particular church because of either birth, marriage, or location. To what extent is that true for the members and families of your group?

- Do you agree with the author's description of why we have so many denominations in the U.S.?

CHANGES:
Deeper and wider

35. Are Roman Catholics and Eastern Orthodox Christians part of the ecumenical movement today?

Yes, in many ways! Many Eastern Orthodox Church bodies in the U.S. are members and participants in local and state councils of churches, and all Orthodox bodies, including Oriental Orthodox churches, are members of the World Council of Churches.

Many Roman Catholic parishes are active members of local councils of churches. More than half of all Roman Catholic dioceses in the U.S. are members of regional and state councils of churches. While the Roman Catholic Church does not hold formal membership in the National and World Councils of Churches, a strong degree of cooperation with these councils has developed in the areas of theological studies and national and world relief work, especially since Vatican II.

36. What changes did Vatican II bring about?

The Second Vatican Council (1962-65) was one of the great milestones in Christianity's ecumenical journey. Pope John XXIII called for a spiritual renewal and an updating (*aggiornamento*) of the church in modern times. Often one hears reference to the pre-Vatican II and the post-Vatican II eras. Vatican II marked the end of the era when the Roman Catholic church referred to other Christians as "separated brethren" or worse.

Vatican II's 25-page "Decree on Ecumenism," adopted by the bishops by a vote of 2,054 to 64 on November 20, 1964, began a completely new chapter in that church's relationship with other Christian bodies.

The decree called for all faithful Roman Catholics to "participate in the work of ecumenism, to come together with others in common prayer, to work more closely in projects a common Christian conscience demands for the common good, and to undertake with vigor the task of renewal and reform."

37. How has the ecumenical movement in the U.S. changed during this century?

The movement has gone through several major changes during the past century. These changes are due partly to the broadening composition of America's religious population.

The movement came to include more churches from a wider scope of theological, ethnic, social, and racial backgrounds. Orthodox Church bodies and the historic black churches play a more significant role today.

The increasingly pluralistic nature of our religious population helps to explain why some local councils of churches are now becoming interfaith councils. Some, such as the Dutchess Interfaith Council of Poughkeepsie, N.Y., have operated on a Judeo-Christian basis for many years. Others, like the Interfaith Conference of Metropolitan Washington (D.C.), include participants of many religious faiths and are among more than 40 such organizations in the U.S. today.

38. What changes have taken place in the life and work of the World Council of Churches?

Even more pronounced changes have taken place within the World Council of Churches. A central example is the location of its participants. Starting in 1948 with representatives largely from North America and Western Europe, recent WCC Assemblies indicate a decided shift in membership with more participants from Africa, Asia, and Latin America.

For example, the regional breakdown of delegates at the 1991 Canberra Assembly in Australia was:

The ecumenical movement, both in the U.S. and at the world level, has not only become more inclusive during this century, but it has also involved the churches in ever deeper theological dialogue to attain a greater degree of visible unity and cooperation.

The poor and the oppressed and victims of modern war continue to be subjects of deep concern.

FOR DISCUSSION

- In what ways did Vatican II make a difference in Roman-Catholic Church life, and in Roman Catholic and non-Roman Catholic relationships?

- To what extent does your church reflect the changes taking place in our U.S. population? Why do we tend to be fearful of changes?

- To what degree should the worldwide expansion of the ecumenical movement, which now includes so many more Christian church bodies in other nations, be a blessing?

DIALOGUE:
Sharing with one another

39. In ecumenical circles, what does the word "dialogue" mean?

It means an open and frank discussion of differences and commonalities in order to understand one another. In the history of the human race, many wars have been conducted, and millions of people have been slain as they battled against one another in the name of religion. The "dialogue" method of relating to those of a different religious faith in our ecumenical journey is a great step forward.

A good example of fruitful open dialogues is found in *Regathering: The Church From "They" to "We."* The Christian participants dealt with such questions as:

> How can our ecumenical walk match our ecumenical talk?

> Can we be more than guests at an ecumenical smorgasbord?

> How can we put the jigsaw puzzle of our divisions together to form the Body of Christ?

> Is God trying to produce a church within the churches?

> How can we be more than "lone rangers," or "sideline" observers?

40. In ecumenical dialogues, what are some helpful guidelines?

A remarkable example of guidelines for ecumenical dialogue was expressed, prior to the beginning of Vatican II, by Robert McAfee Brown and Gustave Weigel, SJ.

Dr. Brown and Father Weigel suggested these six "ground rules." They said that each partner must:

1. Believe that the other is speaking in good faith.

2. Have a clear understanding of his or her own faith.

3. Strive for a clear understanding of the faith of the other.

4. Accept responsibility, in humility and penitence, for what each group has done, and is doing, to foster and perpetuate division.

5. Forthrightly face the issues which cause separation, as well as those which create unity.

6. Recognize that all that can be done with the dialogue is to offer it up to God and that the results must be left in God's hands.

Readers will find a fuller and richer account on what is involved in the deeper meaning of dialogue in Michael Kinnamon's book, *Truth and Community*.

41. To what extent have interchurch studies and dialogues been taking place in the U.S.?

Many such church-sponsored official bilateral dialogues have been taking place. Conducted at a deep theological level, these dialogues have greatly increased during the last several decades. Currently, they are taking place throughout the Christian household. Many denominations are involved in more than a half dozen such dialogues among nearly all branches of Protestantism, the Roman Catholic Church and the Eastern Orthodox churches.

Each bilateral dialogue is at a different point, as the theological leaders of these various church bodies explore ways to attain the fulfillment of Jesus' prayer that his followers may be one. Similar dialogues have been taking place also at the international level between "families" of churches such as Anglican and Roman Catholic.

42. What do the terms "Bilateral" and "Multilateral" dialogues mean?

A bilateral dialogue is a conversation between two parties or traditions only, while a multilateral dialogue involves a number of participants.

While a few serious bilateral dialogues took place prior to the organization of the World and National Councils of Churches, multilateral dialogues greatly increased for a period.

Then in the 1960s there was a new surge of bilateral dialogues which now are beginning to involve almost every branch of the larger Christian family.

The Evangelical Lutheran Church in America, for example, has been or is presently in dialogue with each of the following: Roman Catholics, Anglicans (Episcopalians), Presbyterians, United Church of Christ, Reformed Church in America, United Methodist Church, the Eastern Orthodox churches, Moravian Church, Baptists, and the African Methodist Episcopal Church.

Roman Catholics are in bilateral dialogues with practically all of the other churches listed above, plus the Polish National Catholic Church and the Oriental Orthodox churches.

Episcopalians are in such dialogues with the Roman Catholic Church, the Old Catholic Church, the Evangelical Lutheran Church in America, the Reformed Episcopal Church, the Orthodox churches, and share in conversations with the other eight denominations of the Consultation on Church Union (COCU).

The United Methodist Church is in such dialogues with Lutherans, Roman Catholics, Episcopalians and has been engaged in special conversations with the African Methodist Episcopal Church, the African Methodist Episcopal Zion Church, and the Christian Methodist Church, as well as with the other denominations in COCU.

The United Church of Christ and the Christian Church (Disciples) are sharing in plans in which they would serve as "Partner Churches," in addition to their COCU relationships.

Other denominations are involved in similar official dialogues and conversations.

Such dialogues seek to overcome divisive matters inherited from the past, and to reach agreements on those issues which could bring about a closer fellowship and ministry.

Multilateral dialogues, on the other hand, deal with the broader themes of the Christian faith from a number of viewpoints, but do so as the partners reflect a greater awareness of their common responsibilities in today's society and world.

COCU is probably the best example of the "multilateral" dialogue. Starting in 1962 nine denominations (including three predominantly black churches) started conversations which, it was hoped, would lead to institutional merger. Following an intensive study process within all of the churches between 1968 and 1973 it became clear, however, that this kind of a union was not acceptable to all of the denominations. Consequently, new forms of formal agreement or "covenanting" with one another were developed and are now being voted upon.

43. Have these dialogues produced encouraging results?

Yes and no. Many have been very helpful in clarifying some of the differences between churches. They have frequently led to agreements that some differences which were important in the past should not be church-dividing today. Dialogues have reached some conclusions on conditions that must be met for greater degrees of Christian unity. When churches gradually and mutually receive the results of ecumenical dialogues, the key term for such acceptance is "reception."

Such dialogues have brought about a number of mergers or unions within denominational families in the U.S., and the creation of new church bodies such as the United Church of Canada (1925), and the Church of South India (1947).

The process of "reception" calls for great patience and

courage. In the U.S., John T. Ford and Darlis J. Swan report 12 case studies which describe the degree of "reception" given by 12 congregations to the long series of multilateral ecumenical dialogues which formally produced the 1982 "Baptism, Eucharist, and Ministry" text in Lima, Peru.

Four case studies were each related to baptism, eucharist, and ministry.

None of these stories can be said to be complete, because ecumenism itself is a continuing process. They indicate clearly, however, the long and difficult journey ahead if we are to realize the unity we have been given in Jesus Christ.

Perhaps the most discouraging aspect of the dialogue process is the long delay which has taken place between the conclusions reached by the dialogue participants—often after many years of scholarly study and research—and action by denominational administrative leaders and legislative bodies.

44. Why do some Christians and churches fear such dialogues and the ecumenical movement generally?

Such fear may be based upon a deep misunderstanding of what the ecumenical movement is all about, or a conviction of such Christians or churches that they have the only true interpretation of God's word and God's will. Consequently, many fear that the purity of their doctrines will be watered down or compromised through dialogue, or are so focused on the truth in their own denominations they see no need to dialogue with other Christians about the churches' mission or unity.

"Evangelicals," "conservatives," or "fundamentalist" Christians within these groups tend to place a greater emphasis on a literal interpretation of the Bible, a strong emphasis on the individual's experience of conversion and regeneration, and a deep religious piety. In their earlier history, they had practically no relationship with political activities, but this has changed in more recent times as they have become politically more engaged in opposition to abortion, efforts to insure the civil rights of homosexuals, the teaching of biological evolution to the exclusion of "creationism," and the elimination of prayer in the public schools.

The worldwide consciousness of evangelicals was sharpened considerably, however, when the non-denominational International Congress on World Evangelization was held in Lausanne, Switzerland, in 1974.

Sponsored in part by the Billy Graham Evangelistic Association, this congress brought together almost 2,500 participants from some 150 nations for 10 days of intentional focus on the unfinished task of world evangelization.

A second congress, held in 1989 in Manila, was attended by nearly 3,600 from 170 nations, and increased attention was given to the social implications of the Gospel and its proclamation.

A more recent expression of non-denominational activity has been the Promise Keepers Movement, which at large stadium rallies has emphasized the leadership role of men in strengthening their families and churches.

All ecumenically minded Christians have frequently found, however, that where there is mutual respect for one another as fellow Christians, and where there is the opportunity for the cultivation of personal Christian fellowship, dialogue is not only possible, but can indeed be quite fruitful.

45. What kind of opportunities do we face when we learn about other churches and faiths?

There are at least five:

1. That we may be led to change our own misunderstanding of the Christian faith itself;

2. That we may have to do a lot of homework to interpret our own faith to others;

3. That we may need to correct some of our own misunderstandings about a different church's faith;

4. That we may actually have to heal and repair some of

the damage we have caused others because of our limited vision and understanding;

5. That we may discover how some of our historic church divisions could be healed.

46. Can such dialogues with others lead us to a deeper understanding of our own faith?

It can indeed! This is because many of us have never been well grounded in understanding the deeper dimensions of our own faith and religious heritage, or we have grown rusty and tend to forget. Unless we are prepared to know our own church, we will find it difficult to understand a different church. We must be able to talk about our own church in a way another person can understand. At the same time we may be challenged to look beyond our stereotypes of other faith traditions and discover a richness that can enhance our own faith.

47. When we share in such dialogues, do we have to accept the beliefs of other churches?

No. The purpose of such dialogues is not to convert others to one's own religious perspectives. It is to deepen mutual understanding of one another's beliefs. Then, as the process develops, we can move toward comparing the things we share, the ways we differ, as well as the degree to which our differences should or should not stand in the way of greater Christian unity and cooperation. Our goal is to move closer to each other. During this process, it helps greatly if we can recognize each other as fellow Christians sharing our experiences on a common journey together.

48. What can be done about our differences?

We must continue mentally and spiritually to wrestle with them. As we deepen our understanding of other points of view, perhaps we will be led to review how we came to the conclusions we hold about our own faith. In the light of new knowledge and understanding, maybe we will see or feel the need for readjusting our point of view. If that happens not only will divided Christians move closer together but all be enriched in knowledge of their faith. Our differences may reflect various aspects of the Gospel. They need not be church-dividing.

49. Does my church's participation in the ecumenical movement mean we will give up our form of worship?

No. The ecumenical movement recognizes the need for a variety of forms of Christian worship. Most forms have grown out of centuries of usage and tradition, have deep roots, and cannot be changed easily. Other forms have grown out of different historical experiences and have come to be meaningful for many Christians. An example is the U.S. black church worship experience. The ecumenical movement has never called for one form of worship. It does encourage us, however, to join with other Christians in common experiences of worship. And liturgy is one area of study and discussion within the ecumenical movement. When we can participate together in the use of the great elements of our Christian faith this can bring greater enrichment and fulfillment to all. We need to work together, not only to recognize each other's baptism, but when we may also come to the Lord's Table together.

50. How can our knowledge of other Christian churches be used constructively?

As we share in a study of other churches we learn about how they came to be. Each has its own historical and theological journey. During that journey, each arrived at certain conclusions which helped to shape the life and practice of that church. If we share in such a study with open minds and hearts, it is quite possible that we will discover some developments which could very well enrich our own church and our daily lives as Christians.

51. To what degree, within the framework of the ecumenical movement, can Christians cooperate with persons of other faiths?

Traditionally, this has been a very sensitive subject. When such an approach was first suggested, it was feared to be "syncretism"—the effort to combine or reconcile different beliefs about religion—and was looked upon in a negative way.

Later, it was recognized that Christians could confer with and relate to persons of other faiths in ways that could be non-threatening to each other, and which could be mutually enlightening.

This led then to a variety of conversations such as those with Jews and Muslims whose purpose was not to convert one another to the other faith but was to deepen understanding of each other's faith. Such dialogues have been sponsored by the Roman Catholic Church as well as by the National and World Councils of Churches.

52. How do interfaith relationships differ from Christian ecumenical dialogues?

The theological base for most councils of churches is built upon a common faith in Jesus Christ. The National Council of Churches, for example, is described as a "community of Christian communions" which, "in response to the gospel revealed in the Scriptures, confess Jesus Christ, the incarnate word of God, as Savior and Lord. These communions covenant with one another to manifest ever more fully the unity of the church. Relying upon the transforming power of the Holy Spirit, the Council brings these communions with common mission, serving in all creation to the glory of God." The basis for membership in the World Council of Churches, to which all member churches express their agreement, is described as "a fellowship of churches which confess the Lord Jesus Christ as God and Savior according to the Scriptures and therefore seek to fulfill together their common calling to the glory of the one God, Father, Son and Holy Spirit."

Most state and local councils of churches contain a similar Christ-centered, Trinitarian theological basis for membership.

But a growing number of metropolitan areas, and some cities, are moving toward the development of interfaith organizations. This trend is a response to the increasing pluralistic nature of our religious society as well as a way the total religious community can deal more effectively with complex social problems which face today's world. It is also seen as a way by which a deeper understanding and appreciation can be developed between people of all religious faiths.

In view of these differing goals, many cities have both an interchurch council of churches and an interfaith organization as well.

FOR DISCUSSION

- In what ways are the guidelines for interchurch dialogue helpful? What would you add from your experience?

- What are some of the problems members and pastors of mainline churches face when dialogues are attempted with clergy and lay leaders of the evangelical or fundamentalist churches?

- Just what is required if we are to eliminate our prejudices toward other Christians?

SOCIAL ISSUES:
Relating to the neighbor

53. To what extent do ecumenical and interfaith organizations deal with human needs?

To a considerable extent. While a shift in emphasis is taking place, local councils of churches in the U.S. have given a much larger portion of their efforts and money to meet serious human needs than for Christian unity efforts.

Council leaders tend to take very seriously Jesus' parable of the Good Samaritan (Luke 10:25-37) and his blessings given those who feed the hungry and meet their thirst, welcome the stranger, clothe the naked, and visit the sick and the imprisoned (Matt. 25:31-40).

Consequently, an activity list of both local and state councils of churches and interfaith organizations in the U.S. reveal an amazing number of services and projects.

It is usually easier to begin a partnership on these levels than on the level of theological agreement.

54. What are some examples of how ecumenical councils of churches and interfaith agencies meet such needs?

The list is almost endless. Such programs grow out of serious needs in our different communities. More than 100 such programs—under 10 categories—are being carried out in the U.S. The wide variety of these ministries—which include economic and social concerns, cross-cultural challenges, and events specifically furthering Christian unity—shows ways cooperative agencies seek to bear a common witness. A detailed list of possible programs is in Appendix B.

As we work cooperatively, it is good to remember the principle that we should do together all things, except those which deep differences of conviction compel us to do separately.

55. Should our ecumenical organizations feel a responsibility for helping to shape the moral and ethical qualities of our society?

Definitely! In most of our local communities, if such organizations do not do so, who will? In many cases, our various denominations at the national level have taken positions on many of the issues which are designed to create a more positive and constructive society.

Too often, however, these positions are not implemented at our local or state levels by a local support system. This calls for ecumenically minded clergy and laity on boards of various councils of churches who have vision and courage, to fulfill the prophetic function of Christ's Gospel and to be the leaven which will help to shape our culture so it will more clearly reflect what Jesus called the kingdom of God.

Christ's gospel has both personal and social implications and there must be times when such boards must be advocates for needed social change.

56. How can controversial social issues be handled ecumenically?

For what often appear to be equally valid reasons, Christians will differ strongly on many social issues. Such issues must be handled with sensitive minds and hearts. Just because we differ, however, does not mean that we should avoid dealing with such issues.

How, then, should we handle ecumenically such matters as pro-choice/pro-life positions related to abortion, the civil rights of homosexual persons, war and peace positions, the death penalty, and other equally sensitive social issues?

Councils do this in four ways:

1. Some take a position on what they perceive to be the Christian mind and conscience and try to reach a strong consensus. They do not act until they reach such a consensus.

This can be a very time-consuming process which calls for continued education and dialogue.

2. When such a consensus cannot be reached, councils sometimes agree to issue a statement which presents both sides fairly. This can be a very timely and positive educational contribution to the wider community. One example is the guidelines adopted by the New Mexico Conference of Churches.

3. When agreements cannot be reached, some councils conclude each side must "agree to disagree" and go on as their beliefs lead them. This should be done without bitterness and with respect for those who hold a different position. Our differences should not break the deeper ties which bind us together as fellow Christians.

4. Religious leaders in several cities such as Buffalo, St. Louis, and Pensacola have developed a plan to bring together persons who, for example, hold different positions on the abortion issue. They aim to meet and talk in a non-adversarial way. Their purpose is not to convince or convert one another on the issue of abortion, but to attain a goal of listening, sharing, and understanding.

57. Can governing boards of ecumenical agencies speak out on controversial issues without first securing the backing of their respective church members or denominations?

Yes, provided they speak as an action of their board only. They should never speak as a voice for their member churches or denominations. But there are times when they should speak as boards.

In many cases, our ecumenical agencies can be quite prophetic in applying the principles of Christ's gospel to contemporary needs and problems. Board members should be guided by their insights and understanding of what Christ's Gospel requires, as they are guided by the Holy Spirit.

FOR DISCUSSION

- What is your reaction to the long list of ecumenical activities in Appendix B?

- What kind of social issues should ecumenical organizations speak and act upon?

- How should we handle extremely divisive social issues?

STRUCTURES:
Building plans

58. How are agencies within the ecumenical movement organized and structured?

They are created by their member churches and denominations. In a general way, one can say that local councils of churches are created and supported by local parishes and congregations. State, regional and national councils are created by denominational church bodies. At every level churches elect or select persons to serve on ecumenical agency governing boards. The Ecumenical "E" below should help to clarify these relationships:

CODE:

The Vertical line represents different levels of denominational church life, while the horizontal lines represent various levels of ecumenical relationships.

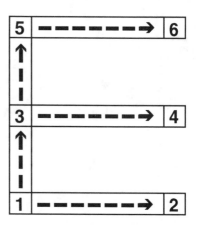

Number "1" represents local parishes and congregations who cooperate to create and serve ecumenically through their local council of churches in #2.

The same local churches in #1 are a part of their state or regional denominational body in #3. These denominational regional bodies in #3 than help to create and serve ecumenically through their state council of churches or their regional ecumenical agencies in #4.

These regional denominational bodies in #3, are also involved in the life of their national denominational body in #5. It is these national denominational bodies who then help to create and serve ecumenically through their national and world councils of churches in #6.

We need to remember, however, that in the broad "fabric" of ecumenism the different levels from local to national—often interact with each other.

59. How are agencies financed?

They are supported basically by their member congregations and denominations. But in view of the large responsibilities councils of churches are asked to carry, such support is hardly ever adequate.

Consequently, most councils must seek additional funding from ecumenically and community-minded individuals, firms and foundations. Some also stage community fund-raising events.

If we sincerely believe that our councils of churches are serving to fulfill the will of our Lord, then we must provide more adequate financial support for their life and operation.

60. What is their most serious problem?

In the opinion of the author, the most serious problem is the dim ecumenical vision of many of today's clergy, and of an even greater number of men and women lay leaders.

The influence of men and women who become strong ecumenical leaders is contagious. The priority they give to the challenge for greater Christian unity and cooperation becomes the solid foundation for fulfillment of our Lord's prayer that "all may be one." When such clergy and lay leadership is encouraged and developed, then other serious problems can be resolved.

FOR DISCUSSION

- How can we provide more adequate financial support for our ecumenical agencies?

- One local council of churches frequently carries this slogan in its monthly newsletter: "The Council Is Your Church—Extended in Mission!" What does that slogan really mean?

THE FUTURE:
Planning for tomorrow

61. What is the long-range future of the ecumenical movement?

There can surely be no question about the continued flow of this movement. As long as there are living Christians there will be an ecumenical movement. Its fulfillment is clearly our Lord's will. Every Christian is called to respond.

As we think about the future, we must remind ourselves of the long struggle through which the movement for greater unity has passed. We then need to compare the progress which has been made in recent times with the nearly 2,000-year history of the Christian church.

Father Thomas Ryan, csp, says that during the last 25 years more progress has been made in Protestant-Roman Catholic relationships than in the previous 450 years. And he says that communications between Eastern Orthodox Christians and Roman Catholic Christians are better than they have been for 900 years.

The big question before every Christian leader is this: Will we permit this call to take priority over so many of the "nuts and bolts" activities which seem to be required to operate our congregations and denominations, and which now receive so much of our time, energy and money?

We grew up and have lived in our divided churches and denominations for so long that we think of this stage of the church's life as being "normal." Such thinking leads some Christians to believe that ecumenism is abnormal. Could it be, that in God's sight, the reverse is true? If so, then, as Father Ryan has said, "We live in a pre-ecumenical age, not a post-ecumenical retreat."

62. Do theological seminaries need a stronger curriculum on the history, purposes, and developments within the ecumenical movement?

While the winds of the Spirit flow in many directions, much of the future for the ecumenical movement in the U.S. is now being determined by our theological seminaries.

It is here that the spiritual leaders for the future are trained. Are they motivated to explore the amazing ecumenical developments which have taken place in this century? Do they intentionally explore Jesus' will for greater Christian unity and its implications?

A recent survey, made by the Pennsylvania Council of Churches of the seminaries in that state and by the National Workshop on Christian Unity, indicates that most seminary curricula are very weak in this respect.

At a recent national ecumenical conference an ecumenical leader of some 40 years said, "I became interested in Christian unity because, as I was growing up, my pastor preached strongly on this theme. I haven't heard such a sermon in my church for the last five years."

Can our seminaries help to provide the ecumenical leaders needed to inspire and motivate our laity for greater ecumenical leadership tomorrow?

A partial answer to that question can be seen in the rise of a series of theological consortia. A number of seminaries establish a partnership arrangement whereby students from any one of a number of cooperating area seminaries may cross-register for credit courses in other seminaries, sometimes without paying additional course fees. Such consortia are made up of Roman Catholic, Protestant, and Orthodox seminaries located in such areas as Atlanta, Berea (KY), Berkeley (CA), Boston, Chicago, Kerrville (TX), Lexington (KY), Minneapolis/St. Paul, New York, Richmond, Rochester, and Washington, D.C.

63. How can I learn more about the ecumenical movement?

If you've read this far, you've made a good beginning. If you live in a community where there is a council of churches, an interfaith organization, or a ministerial association—which often carries out some of the functions of a council of churches—you may want to talk further with an officer.

Be encouraged to know there are between 600 and 700 local, state and regional councils of churches and church-based community ministries in the United States, including 47 state councils of churches. Many of these go by various names: councils or conferences of churches, ecumenical councils, churches united, metropolitan ministries, etc. But all are engaged in a wide variety of ecumenical ministries.

This handbook may have inspired you to do more reading on this subject. Books marked with an asterisk in the bibliography are helpful starting points. They could also be a resource for a study group in your church or community.

Many denominations also have national ecumenical officers. Your local pastor should have the name and address.

Most denominational publishing houses also offer study resources on such subjects as "Your Neighbor's Faith." Your pastor, or a neighboring pastor, may also have recommendations.

64. How can I become ecumenically involved?

That should be easy! Speak to your pastor or one or two of your ecumenical council or council of churches leaders. Tell them of your interest and your willingness to serve as a volunteer where you are needed. Get acquainted with others who have the same spirit. Learn about the ecumenical opportunities which exist in your area. Review the long list of ecumenical events and ministries being conducted and carried out by other councils of churches. (See Appendix B).

You can encourage your church to be involved in working with other churches in a wide range of ecumenical activities. Are there crying needs in your community which the churches ought to try to meet together? Would you like to try to start some needed service? Do church people in your community need to have a better understanding of one another?

65. How can my participation in the ecumenical movement enrich my Christian Faith?

You may be surprised about how such participation will enrich your spiritual life. It will surely broaden your religious outlook. It will help you understand some of the wider dimensions of the Christian faith and how other Christians feel about things which are important to you. It may free you from some old prejudices and help you develop new appreciations. But these enriched blessings are only possible if you can share in such relationships with an open mind and heart.

Perhaps this letter from a lay woman will encourage you. She was a former member of a very isolationist denomination and wrote this after agreeing to serve on the board of directors of the local council of churches:

> "When I was invited to become a board member of our council of churches, I hesitated. Frankly, I had never heard of such an organization in any of the many places I had lived. With a 35-year history in my former denomination, I fretted about how negative I might be. I doubted that a group of people with diverse doctrines and practices could ever come to a positive agreement on efforts which might be helpful to the community. I expected a lot of clashing and gnashing of teeth.
>
> "In my three years on this board, I witnessed very little of this. I learned that Board members must show an example of 'oneness' in their decisions. I soon learned and saw how both clergy and lay people

brought the needed balance.

"I discovered that churches working together, like our council, can become a great clearing and steering house for our community. We can launch bigger and better projects than each denomination going it alone.

"Joint worship efforts, too, have provided opportunities to become more understanding of other denominations and cultures. Some of us have had little exposure to diversity. Diverse cultures do not come to us, and we rarely go out looking for them.

"As Bishop Tutu has said, 'Too often, we take the soft option, and paper over the cracks.'

"It was amazing to discover how we could hold hands together in many of our ecumenical efforts as we traveled along rightful paths."

66. How can ecumenical participation enrich the life of my congregation?

Encourage your pastor to form a leadership team of like-minded ecumenists in your congregation who are willing to reach out to other congregations in your community. If such relationships are well established and developed, it will help to destroy the competitive feeling toward other churches which often exists. Instead of being competitors you will gradually feel like Christian partners who are jointly trying to fulfill the mission of Christ. The life of your congregation and your community can be greatly enriched by such ecumenical participation.

This will be especially true if your church can cooperate with other churches in joint service projects, study groups and prayer or worship services.

In these ways, you will come to pray for one another, rather than to belittle or quarrel with one another. Is this not the way of our Lord?

Review where your congregation stands in these "5-C"

ecumenical stages of ecumenical outlook:

1. *Competition.* This is a pre-ecumenical stage in which the church sees itself as being entirely self-sufficient. It is the "Lone Ranger" style of operation.

2. *Coexistence.* In this stage, the church acknowledges the presence of Christ in other churches, but no steps are taken to work together.

3. *Cooperation* recognizes a limited partnership between churches to work together in particular ministries.

4. *Commitment* or *Covenanting* involves deeper ecumenical ties, and a willingness to explore the differences between churches as well as the desire to work for greater unity. It could involve the promise to remember each other in prayer, choir exchanges and special common services of worship.

5. *Communion.* This stage takes place when (a) different branches within a tradition are able to unite; or (b) when different traditions, such as those which formed the United Church of Christ, agree to unite; or (c) when agreements are reached between such denominations or traditions as Lutheran-Episcopal or Lutheran-Reformed in the sharing of Holy Communion and ministries.

Where is your church in these ecumenical stages?

67. Should we pray for the success of this movement?

By all means! Since prayer is our inner, personal and corporate communication with God, as well as God's way of communicating with us, such prayer is indeed basic. In our prayers, we tend to include those matters which will be closest to our hearts and for which we need and seek God's will. Prayer changes hearts, and it is our hearts that need to be changed. Surely it is God's will that all Christians should live in greater harmony. If that is a heart-felt need, then we must pray for its fulfillment. Some may wish to use the Ecumenical Prayer Cycle, available through the World Council of Churches, which enables Christians to pray for all other Christians during a 52-week cycle of prayers from every part of the earth.

The Annual Week of Prayer for Christian Unity (January 18-25) is another splendid opportunity for the congregations of every local community.

Let us not forget James 5:16, "The prayer of the righteous is powerful and effective."

68. Will my pastor be supportive?

Let us hope and pray that your pastor will be supportive of your ecumenical hopes and dreams. We must realize, however, that the spiritual goals of pastors—like our own spiritual goals—are shaped and determined by past religious experiences, theological study, and prayer. Consequently, because our backgrounds vary, not all pastors share the same spiritual goals. This means that you must be prepared to work toward understanding with your pastor so that you both can work toward fulfilling God's will for greater Christian unity.

69. Is there a common symbol for the ecumenical movement?

While no one symbol can be said officially to represent the ecumenical movement, variations of the WCC symbol do appear in various places.

The center of that symbol is usually a ship, an historic symbol of the church. Rising as a mast above the ship is a cross, which symbolizes the presence and power of Christ in determining the movement and direction of the ship. Beneath the ship are several curved lines which portray the waves—the trials and tribulations of life—to which the church must always be related. Above all of this is often one word: OIKOUMENE, the Greek word for Ecumenical.

The entire symbol is often enclosed in a circle, which represents the all inclusiveness of the ecumenical movement.

In looking at this symbol, however, we must never forget that while Christ is the central power—the captain—for moving the church, the ship still needs a human crew to carry out his commands. We can each be a part of that crew!

70. To what degree is the ecumenical movement called to help shape the culture of today's world?

As Christians, we believe the values of the Christian Gospel can help greatly to resolve the serious problems which confront and afflict today's human family. These problems are deep-rooted. Every newscast and daily paper carries stories which seem to threaten our very survival. The breakdown of family life, and especially the growing number of single parents; the increase of violence, including even the use of guns by children; the rise in crime and overflowing prisons; the broader usage of alcohol and drugs; the widespread, long-standing and destructive wars between peoples; massive deaths all over the world from starvation, and the growing millions of refugees—all these cause us to ponder: How can we change the shape of our communities, our nation, our world?

There can be no doubt that a greater unity among Christians is God's will as we understand it in the life and teaching of Jesus Christ.

It is also clear that our present excessive divisions have greatly weakened our total Christian witness both in this country and throughout the world.

These divisions are both shameful and sinful. Every denomination has more than its share of human self-centeredness and long, historical inclinations for institutional self-preservation.

Truly, this is a time to recall the words of John 3:16, "For God so loved the world that he gave his only Son, so that everyone who believes may not perish, but may have eternal life."

71. Is there a parting word?

It is that we should never forget the prayer of our Lord that we may be one, even as Jesus and the Father are one, that the "world may believe" (John 17:21).

This is a time to hear again the words of Jesus: "I came that you might have life and have it more abundantly" (John 10:10).

Surely, none of our churches, nor any one of our denominations, can change the crippled state of today's world. But there is a reasonable chance of doing so, if we—the Christians of the world—can live, pray, and work together.

FOR DISCUSSION

- To what degree is your local congregation involved in the ecumenical movement? How is your denomination involved?

- What can the churches of your community do together to strengthen your community's weaknesses and negative influences?

- How can your congregation bear a stronger ecumenical witness in your community, your denomination, and the world?

APPENDIX A
Pioneers of the modern ecumenical movement

1.   JOHN R. MOTT (1865-1955), a U.S. Methodist layman who probably did more than any one person to lay the foundations for what was to become the World Council of Churches in 1948. His outstanding leadership, through the Student Christian Movement, inspired many other leaders to follow him and led one writer to say that in the cause of world evangelization, he was "as tireless and as urgent as the Apostle Paul." He was chairman of the 1910 International Missionary Conference and received the Nobel Peace Prize in 1946.

2.   NATHAN SODERBLOM (1866-1931) was the strong Lutheran Archbishop of Sweden who brought together the Universal Christian Conference on Life and Work held in Stockholm in 1925. Coming after World War I, it was a major step in helping the churches face their common Christian responsibility to bring humanity together in peace, and to work for greater degrees of justice within and between the nations.

3.   CHARLES H. BRENT (1862-1929), Episcopal Bishop of Western New York, prepared and chaired the Christian World Conference on Faith and Order held at Lausanne, Switzerland in 1927. The conference paved the way for many theological dialogues which followed in succeeding decades among various branches of Christendom. These dialogues dealt with possible agreements on some of the essential elements of Christian faith and order—the manner that faith should be expressed in the life and structure of the different church bodies and traditions.

Another Episcopalian, the Rev. Paul James Wattson, Graymoor, N.Y.—after becoming a Roman Catholic—helped to launch, in 1906, what became the worldwide Week of Prayer for Christian Unity.

4. JOSEPH H. OLDHAM (1874-1969), English Anglican layman and scholar whose creative ecumenical thinking and whose writings laid foundations for the rise of the ecumenical movement in the 20th century. He was named an honorary president of the World Council of Churches in 1948. Perhaps it could be said he was the Thomas Jefferson of the ecumenical movement.

5. WILLEM VISSER'T HOOFT (1900-1985), strong international YMCA leader, who was later ordained a minister in the Netherlands Reformed Church, was the first General Secretary of the World Council of Churches. He served in this capacity between 1948 and 1968 and was the guiding light during these decades of growth. He is credited to be the leading figure of the 20th century ecumenical movement.

6. GEORGES FLOROVSKY (1893-1979), from the Ukraine, served as a universally recognized Orthodox spokesman in the early days of the ecumenical movement. He helped bridge some of the gaps created by the great division between eastern and western Christians which took place in 1054 A.D.

7. SAMUEL McCREA CAVERT (1888-1975), after serving as secretary to the student YMCA movement, became a Presbyterian minister and played a very influential role in the development of plans for U.S. participation in the 1948 Assembly of the World Council of Churches. He served as the general secretary of the U.S. Federal Council of Churches (1951-54), and as the executive secretary of the U.S. office of the World Council of Churches (1954-57).

8. EUGENE CARSON BLAKE (1906-1985), an American Presbyterian leader, was president of the U.S.

National Council of Churches (1954-57) and served as the general secretary of the World Council of Churches (1966-72). In 1960, he made a proposal for a multi-lateral Consultation on Church Union which came to include nine U.S. denominations, including three predominantly African American church bodies. All were challenged to explore the establishment of a church that would be "truly catholic, truly evangelical, and truly reformed."

9. CYNTHIA CLARK WEDEL (1908-1986) was an associate general secretary of the U.S. National Council of Churches (1960-69) and a president of the World Council of Churches (1975-83). An Episcopalian from Virginia, she served also as a president of Church Women United.

Strong ecumenical leadership was also provided by such women as Annie R. Jiagge of Ghana, Nita Barrow, Barbados, and Lois Miriam Wilson, Canada, who also served as World Council presidents.

10. JOHN XXIII (1881-1963), Pope of the Roman Catholic Church (1958-63), is best known ecumenically for calling the Second Vatican Council (1962-65) and for the council's "Decree on Ecumenism." This marked the beginning of more specific ecumenical participation of the Roman Catholic Church, a step which had been resisted for more than 50 years. This was truly an historical milestone in the ecumenical journey.

The list of such ecumenical pioneers could, of course, be doubled or tripled. Some of the author's ecumenical colleagues have suggested these additions:

INDIA: D. T. Niles (1908-70); M. M. Thomas (1916-); Leslie Newbigin (1909-).

GERMANY: Otto Dibelius (1880-1967); Hans Lilje (1899-1977); Martin Niemoller (1892-1987).

FRANCE: Marc Boegner (1881-1970); Madeleine Barot (1909-); Suzanne de Dietrich (1891-1981).

ENGLAND: George Bell (1883-1958); Ernest Payne (1902-1980); Pauline Webb (1927-).

SCOTLAND: John Alexander Mackey (1889-1983).

GREECE: Athenagoras I (1886-1972).

SOUTH AMERICA: David J. Du Plessis (1905-1987).

CZECHOSLOVAKIA: Joseph Hromadka (1889-1970).

RUSSIA: Boris Nikodim (1929-1978).

UNITED STATES: Samuel S. Schmucker (1779-1873); Henry Knox Sherill (1890-1980); Franklin Clark Fry (1900-1968); G. Bromley Oxnam (1891-1963).

It is probably safe to say that within every Christian tradition and during each century of the Christian era there have been leaders who have dreamed and worked for the greater oneness of all Christians. We are the recipients of their labors.

APPENDIX B

Here are some 100 programs and ways councils of churches and interfaith agencies seek to meet human needs and achieve greater degrees of visible unity. To what extent can or should some of these programs be carried out in your community?

I. FAMILY-RELATED NEEDS:

1. Child abuse prevention program
2. Child care assistance
3. Runaway and homeless youth
4. Sexual exploitation of youth
5. Adolescent pregnancy
6. Teen moms infant care
7. Group home for girls
8. Coats for kids
9. Back-to-school clothing assistance
10. Christmas toy sales
11. Share-a-toy at Christmas
12. Low-income store
13. Used clothing distribution
14. Family violence
15. Ministry to the aging
16. Mothers' aides
17. Convalescent sitters
18. Assistance to homebound shoppers
19. Marriage and family life
20. Spouse abuse
21. Battered women shelters

II. EDUCATION-RELATED NEEDS:

1. Tutoring programs
2. Boy Scout/Girl Scout religious awards

3. Teen pregnancy prevention
4. International student hospitality
5. Mentally ill assistance
6. Mentally handicapped assistance
7. Elimination of pornography
8. Christian sports
9. Schools of religion
10. Campus ministries

III. JOB-RELATED NEEDS:

1. Job training
2. Summer youth employment
3. Migrant and farmworker ministries
4. Job banks for unemployed

IV. MEDICAL-RELATED NEEDS:

1. Blood donor coordination
2. Alcoholism education
3. Substance abuse prevention
4. Hospital chaplaincies
5. AIDS chaplaincies
6. Cancer and AIDS hospices
7. Free medical and dental clinics
8. Hearing aid bank
9. Interreligious health care

V. FOOD-RELATED NEEDS:

1. CROP walks
2. UNICEF drives
3. Soup kitchens
4. Food banks and pantries
5. Meals-on-Wheels

VI. HOUSING-RELATED NEEDS:

1. Emergency Shelters

2. Hospitality for homeless
3. Housing for Low-Income Families
4. Habitat-For-Humanity
5. Emergency Fuel Bank
6. High-Rise Apartment Ministry

VII. CROSS-CULTURAL NEEDS:

1. Combatting Racism
2. Martin Luther King, Jr. Day Celebration
3. Hispanic Heritage
4. Cross-Cultural Programs: African-American, Hispanic, Native American
5. Refugee-Support Services

VIII. PRISON-RELATED NEEDS:

1. Yokefellow Prison Ministry
2. Prison Visitation Programs
3. Prison Chaplains
4. Police Department Chaplains

IX. CHRISTIAN UNITY PROJECTS:

1. Week of Prayer for Christian Unity
2. Ecumenical Dialogues
3. COCU Conferences (Consultation on Church Union)
4. BEM Studies (Baptism, Eucharist and Ministry)
5. Weekly Ecumenical Luncheons
6. Pre-Lenten Celebration
7. Weekly Lenten Services
8. Joint Good Friday Services
9. Easter Dawn Services
10. Ecumenical Thanksgiving
11. Ecumenical Advent Prayer Breakfast
12. Religious Christmas Parade
13. Ecumenical Pentecost Service
14. Messiah Community Sing

15. Ecumenical Music Celebrations
16. Ecumenical Hymn Festivals
17. Ecumenical Choir Camp
18. Festivals of Faith
19. Reformation/Reconciliation Services
20. Mayor's Prayer Breakfast
21. Church Women United
22. Pulpit Exchanges
23. Bible Distributions
24. Common Ecumenical Lectionary Studies

X. SPECIAL PROJECTS:

1. Airport Chaplaincy Services
2. Truck Stop Chaplaincy
3. State & National Park Chaplaincies
4. Disaster Response Preparation
5. Flood Relief Network
6. Shepherd of the Streets Urban Ministry
7. State Fair Ministries
8. Metro Paint-A-Thon
9. U.S./Canadian Border Concerns
10. Witness For Peace
11. Peace With Justice
12. World Peace & Global Affairs
13. Ecology Task Force
14. Economic Justice Issues
15. Joint Religious Legislative Coalition
16. Radio & TV Ministries
17. Common Ground Coalition
18. Church Purchasing Cooperatives
19. Holocaust Memorial observance
20. Christian/Jewish Conversations
21. Christian/Muslim Conversations
22. World Relief Projects

APPENDIX C

From Thomas Ryan's Forward Movement pamphlet
"What Does It Mean to Be Ecumenical?"

Recently a friend asked the same question. It was one of those queries that stops you cold because the answer goes off in so many directions you don't know where to begin. Later, as an exercise for myself, I took paper and pencil in hand and began to reflect on the lessons of my last twelve years in ecumenical work.

What does it mean to be ecumenical? Colleagues with more years of experience will surely supplement what follows, but these are some of the things which, in my experience, "being ecumenical" means:

1. To pray regularly for the unity of the Church: As Christ wills it and when he wills it. As theologian Yves Congar said, "The way through the door of unity is on our knees." Prayer is important because prayer's effect is in us. Prayer changes our hearts, and it is our hearts that most of all need to be changed.

2. To be rooted in a particular Christian tradition: To know it well, and to be able to present the coherency of that tradition's response to the Gospel to others. The genuine ecumenists are not at the margin of their church's life, but at the heart of it. They know what is important in the Christian life, and can recognize those elements in other churches even if they may be differently expressed.

3. To take an active part in the careful and honest appraisal of whatever needs to be done for the renewal of one's own church: Ecumenism is not a specialty within the church, but an expression of every dimension of its life. It helps the church to be more the church and to be faithful to her calling. Dialogue is the meeting of churches. The purpose

of dialogue is to help one another renew the churches in order to carry out Christ's mission for his one Church.

4. To be fascinated and curious about that which is different: To risk peeping out of our provincial perspectives and opening ourselves to the bigger picture. Ecumenism is a way of living that dares to think globally and live trustfully with differences in community.

5. To be willing to learn: Truth is seldom discovered in isolation but rather through dialogue in diverse community. Each Christian tradition has preserved better than others one or more aspects of the mystery of God's work in Christ. The work of unity aims at restoring the fullness of our common appreciation of that mystery.

6. To cultivate an historical consciousness: We're on a journey. The church we have is not the church God wants. An ecumenically minded person refuses to worship false gods, and the present expression of the church is not God. Similarly, there is a refusal to make absolute a stage of development which is only the next step on the way to something greater.

7. To be ready to celebrate vitality in the Body of Christ wherever it is found: What advances the reign of God in any church helps all churches. The churches are not like competing corporations in the business world, so that the stakes of one rises as the lot of others falls. Any loss of divine truth and life is a loss to Christ and his Church. The only triumph a Christian seeks is that of Jesus and his cross. Our rivalry is not with one another, but with sin.

8. To be willing to work together: Ecumenism is an understanding of human society that identifies fear of the "other" as one of the greatest evils we face. The principle given to all the churches for their life together is: Do everything together as far as conscience permits.

9. To feel the scandal of our divisions: Unity is for mission. Our primary mission is to announce the good news.

The message we joyfully proclaim is that we are

reconciled to God and to one another through the life, death and resurrection of Jesus. But our divided state as we announce it deprives the message of credibility. "Being ecumenical" means feeling a holy unrest at our failure to live consistently with our message, and more interested in proving our "rightness" and the other's "wrongness" than in seeking together to know what the Spirit is asking of us, and to do it.

10. To be open to God's will for the Church: Our unity in Christ is God's gift, and the way to give more visible expression to that gift will also be God's gift. But we will have to empty ourselves of our self-righteousness and let go of our power games in order to let this be God's work. Our contribution is our willingness to uncover and surrender whatever prevents our being filled with God.

11. To appreciate the important role of provisional regulations and church structures in our evolution from alienation to reconciliation: To accept that the only constant is change, and the only refuge is the insecure security of faith. To struggle against the temptation to live in a closed, same, secure system that reduces our level of fear and satisfies our desires for control. God is a verb. And in the dynamism of the provisional, God's Spirit is at work, endlessly correcting, improving, adjusting, reorienting. Like a pilgrim's tent, our best efforts today must be recognized as provisional and be ready to give way to better forms tomorrow for advancing our life together.

12. To have an appreciation for the hierarchy of truths in Christian doctrine: A belief has greater or lesser consequences in the measure in which it relates to the foundation of the Christian faith. Grace has more importance than sin, the Holy Spirit more than Mary, the mystical aspect of the Church more than its juridical nature, the church's liturgy more than private devotions, baptism more than penance, the Eucharist more than the anointing of the sick. Placing the greater stress on those doctrines in closest relation to

the heart of Christian faith enables-us to build further agreement on the firm foundation we share.

13. To try to understand others as they understand themselves: To avoid any expression, judgment or action that falsifies their condition. Ecumenical honesty means we do not look upon others through the prism of their weakest elements, or over-generalize their positions with statements like, "Protestants say . . . Anglicans do . . . Orthodox are . . . Catholics will . . . " Rather, our ideals are put next to their ideals, our practices next to their practices, as opposed to our ideals next to their practices.

14. To be alert to the presence of God and the action of the Holy Spirit in the lives of other Christians and members of other living faiths: The Church of God does not have a mission as much as the mission of God has a Church. The Church is the sign and sacrament of God's presence in the world, but God's activity is by no means limited to the Church and its members. The Church serves the advance of the Kingdom, but is not tantamount to it.

15. To have a biblical patience: Biblical patience calls for creative waiting, doing now what we can instead of moaning about what church disciplines will not allow us to do. It means being willing to accept or absorb negativity so that the person who is the source of it will eventually go beyond it. Christ suffered for unity. At times so will we. Biblical patience involves staying with it, seeing it through, searching for the healing that comes from understanding and forgiveness. Everyone is in favor of Christian unity. Some are even willing to work for it. But few are willing to suffer for it.

ACKNOWLEDGMENTS

In reviewing the stages which led to this publication, I am deeply indebted to a very widespread corps of dedicated ecumenists who have helped develop, evaluate, and encourage this project.

I especially wish to express my thanks to these ecumenically-minded and dedicated leaders:

John Archer, David Baak, Darold Beekmann, Gwen Bernstine, Dorothy Berry, Joan Brown Campbell, John Confer, Paul Crow Jr., Larue Dieter, Robert Driesen, Thomas Duke, Doris Edwards, William Fleming, Jerry Folk, Charla Grieves, Daniel Hamby, Annabel Hartman, Norman Hjelm, John Hotchkin, Kathleen Hurty, Phillips Jenks, Arleon Kelley, Michael Kinnamon, Daniel Kovalak, Nancy Lady, Peter Laurence, Clark Lobenstine, Damian MacPherson, Judith Marker, Daniel Martensen, Elizabeth Mellon, Willis Merriman, Albert Myers, Barbara Myers, William Norgren, Joan Parrott, Albert Pennybacker, John Piper Jr., Jeanne Audrey Powers, Bruce Robbins, William Rusch, Thomas Ryan, Craig Schaefer, Louise Schaeffer, Warren Strandberg, Jean Stromberg, John Thomas, Herbert Thompson Jr., Willmar Thorkelson, Eugene Turner and Peggy Way.

And this would be most incomplete if it did not include my secretary, Virginia Garver, who faithfully deciphered the hieroglyphics of my longhand copy.

But above all others has been the patient and loving support of my wife, Mildred, whose sense of partnership provided the sustaining motivation and encouragement so necessary to complete this labor of love for the greater oneness of all of God's children.

BIBLIOGRAPHY

NOTE: Resources marked with an asterisk should be very helpful for study group discussion purposes.

Acting In Faith, a 29-minute video by Bill Turpie, New York Office (WCC), 475 Riverside Dr., New York, NY 10115-0050. Interprets the work of the World Council of Churches in various parts of the world where the Council provides insights and commitment to help member churches "act in faith" as the Body of Christ. Konrad Raiser, the WCC General Secretary, is the chief narrator.

An American Dialogue by Robert McAfee Brown and Gustave Weigel, S.G., Anchor Books, Doubleday, New York. 240 pp. 1961.

"Baptism, Eucharist and Ministry," World Council of Churches, Geneva, Switzerland. 33 pp. 1982. A text of a significant ecumenical document of the World Council of Churches, adopted at Lima, Peru in 1982, which summarizes a long 30-year history of study and dialogue on various Christian beliefs and practices related to baptism, the Lord's Supper, and the basis for an ordained ministry.

Dictionary of the Ecumenical Movement, World Council of Churches, Eerdmans, Grand Rapids, MI. 1,196 pp. 1991. This is almost literally a 'Bible' of the ecumenical movement. It includes descriptions of more than 600 alphabetically-arranged subjects, and is an indispensable reference for students, scholars, lay church leaders, and pastors.

Directory for the Application of Principles and Norms on Ecumenism by Pontifical Council For Promoting Christian Unity. U.S. Catholic Conference, Washington, D.C.

100 pp. 1993. An extremely valuable resource for all who want to become better acquainted with where the Roman Catholic stands today in ecumenical matters, and who wish to discover helpful ways of cooperation.

Documents of Vatican II, Walter M. Abbott, s.j., General Editor, The America Press, New York. 791 pp. 1966. Contains the official Decree on Ecumenism and 15 other documents of the history-making sessions of the Roman Catholic Second Vatican Council held in Rome, 1963-1965.

Double Belonging: Interchurch Families and Christian Unity by George Kilcourse, Paulist Press, Ramsey, NJ. 179 pp. 1992. Father Kilcourse, a Catholic theologian, presents the thesis that interchurch couples should not be perceived as a problem for the churches, but as a gift for the restoration of the church's unity.

*Ecumenism—A Movement Toward Church Unity by William G. Rusch. Fortress Press, Minneapolis, MN. 1985. 133 pp. A very readable and highly recommended account of the history and description of the ecumenical movement; the way it functions in councils of churches and in inter-church dialogues; and an evaluation of where it is today and could be tomorrow.

Ecumenism In Transition: A Paradigm Shift in the Ecumenical Movement by Konrad Raiser. World Council of Churches. 132 pages. 1994. A very thoughtful analysis of where the ecumenical movement is today and where it could be going tomorrow. Dr. Raiser is currently the General Secretary of the World Council of Churches.

Growing Together In Baptism, Eucharist and Ministry by William H. Lazareth. World Council of Churches, Geneva, Switzerland. 108 pp. 7th printing. 1985. A thoughtful and challenging study book on BEM—"Baptism, Eucharist and Ministry."

Handbook of Member Churches, compiled by Ans J. van der Bent. 2nd Revised edition. World Council of Churches, Geneva, Switzerland. 283 pp. 1985. A reliable source about the more than 300 church bodies, arranged alphabetically by continents and nations who are members of the World Council of Churches. An invaluable resource.

History of the Ecumenical Movement: Vol. I: 1517-1948, edited by Ruth Rouse and Stephen Charles Neill. *Vol. II: 1948-1968*, edited by Harold E. Fey, World Council of Churches, 4th printing, 1,448 pp. 1993.

Vol. I provides a rich and detailed account of the difficult 400-year Christian unity journey between the Protestant Reformation and the formation of the World Council of Churches.

Vol. II describes the above history for the two decades following the organization of the World Council of Churches in 1948. Now available in one hardback.

How To Survive An Ecumenical Transfusion: A Study of Buffalo Ecumenism In Transition by Alton M. Motter, Buffalo Council of Churches, Buffalo, NY. 73 pp. 1975. An account of how the religious leaders of the city of Buffalo wrestled to determine their ecumenical future.

Hymnal Companion To The Lutheran Book of Worship by Marilyn Kay Stulker, Fortress, Minneapolis, MN. 647 pp. 1981. The text and tune stories back of the 569 hymns in the *Lutheran Book of Worship*.

Memoirs by Willem Adolph Visser't Hooft, Westminster, Philadelphia, PA. 379 pp. 1973. The warm, human stories of the man who, for more than 50 years, was involved in ecumenical church life at national and international levels, and who helped to give shape and direction to the World Council of Churches.

Mid-Stream, Oct. 1993 (Vol. 32 No. 4), "The Drama of Local and Regional Ecumenism in the U.S.," Council on Christian Unity of the Christian Church (Disciples of Christ), Indianapolis, IN. A quarterly publication on phases of the ecumenical movement today.

Practical Guide to Community Ministry by A. David Bos, Westminster/John Knox Press, Louisville, KY. 84 pp. 1993.

Practicing Ecumenism, Liturgical Conference, Silver Spring, MD 20910. A recent practical resource for local ecumenism leaders. 81 pp. 1992.

Regathering: The Church from "They" to "We" by Esther Boyle Bruland, Eerdmans, Grand Rapids, MI. 155 pp. 1995. This is an unusual collection of very personal stories and convictions about ecumenism as 15 people from almost every segment of the Christian family shared their feelings with one another in a series of five consultations at the unique Institute for Ecumenical and Cultural Research at Collegeville, MN. The consultations "mix" included Evangelical, Pentecostal, Holiness Christians, as well as Mainline Protestant, Roman Catholic and Orthodox Christians.

A School for God's People: A history of the Sunday School movement in Indiana by Grover L. Hartman, Central Publishing, Indianapolis, IN. 106 pp. 1980. A very readable description of the rise and role of the Sunday School movement and the way it paved the way for wider forms of church cooperation in the state of Indiana.

Survival Guide for Ecumenically Minded Christians by Thomas Ryan, CSP, Liturgical Press, Collegeville, MN. 163 pp. 1989. One of the best recent books on ecumenism today. Highly recommended for all readers.

Tales of Christian Unity: The Adventures of An Ecumenical Pilgrim by Thomas Ryan, CSP. Paulist Press, Ramsey, NJ. 281 pp. 1983. This is a "must" book for all who would understand the worldwide dimensions and hope for today's ecumenical movement. The Prologue and Epilogue are especially valuable. It is written in a language that lay people will understand.

Truth and Community: Diversity and Its Limits In The Ecumenical Movement, by Michael Kinnamon. Eerdmans, Grand Rapids, MI. 1988. A very valuable resource to gain a deeper awareness of what is involved in Christian ecumenical dialogue.

Together: The Story of Church Cooperation In Minnesota by H.L. Stright, T.S. Denison & Co., Minneapolis, MN. 308 pp. 1971. The account of the 115-year interdenominational history of what became one of the most outstanding state councils of churches in the nation.

*Twelve Tales Untold: A Study Guide for Ecumenical Reception, edited by John T. Ford and Darlis J. Swan, Eerdmans, Grand Rapids, MI. 178 pp. 1993. Describes the successes and difficulties involved in 12 case studies in which congregations dealt with the "reception" of the content of Baptism, Eucharist and Ministry.

Twenty Centuries of Ecumenism, by Canon Jacques Desseau, Paulist Press, Ramsey, NJ. 103 pp. 1984. A very helpful overall survey of the many divisions and movements for reconciliation which have taken place between Christians over the centuries.

United Methodist Hymnal, United Methodist Publishing House, Nashville, TN. 962 pp. 1989. The official Hymnal and Book of United Methodist Worship.

Week of Prayer Resource Booklet, Graymoor Ecumenical &
Inter-religious Institute, Garrison, NY 10524-0300, offers
many helpful suggestions and resources for observing the
annual Jan. 18-25 Week of Prayer for Christian Unity.
Published annually about Sept. 15.

Basic facts, figures, and information can be found in publications such as current copies of the *Encyclopedia Britannica*,
the *World Almanac*, and the *Yearbook of American and Canadian Churches*.

Index